ENGLAND ENGLAND ENGLAND ENGLAND ENGLAND

ENGLAND

ENGLAND

ENGLAND

ENGLAND

ENGLAND

ENGLAND

ENGLAND

First published by Parragon in 2007
Parragon
Queen Street House
4 Queen Street
Bath BA1 1HE, UK

TheFA.com

All information correct at time of creation, April 2007

ISBN 978-1-4075-0439-1

Printed in China

Contents

Phil Neville playing for England against Spain in February 2007

Game On

England are one of the world's most successful football sides. Here we cover all the major tournaments England have entered, as well as taking an in-depth look at their six greatest football rivals.

World Cup

England are one of just seven countries to have won the World Cup. They didn't enter the first three competitions, but when the 1950 tournament came around in Brazil, England were raring to go!

At the time they were considered to be the best side in the world. Then came one of the biggest ever shocks in World Cup history – England lost 1-0 to the USA. Nowadays that would be like losing to a footballing minnow like San Marino or Andorra! They also lost their next game 1-0 to Spain and were soon packing their bags.

World Cup Semi: 27th July 1966: Eusebio of Portugal (left) and Nobby Stiles of England in a duel for the ball during their World Cup semi-final match at Wembley, which England won 2-1. (Photo by Central Press/Getty Images)

The 1954 Finals were held in Switzerland, and once again England sailed through the qualifying group, which was made up of the other home nations, Scotland, Wales and Northern Ireland. They reached the quarter-finals in the end before going out to Uruguay 4-2.

In 1958, the World Cup was staged in Sweden and this was to be the tournament when Brazil first showed their flair and brilliance. As for England, they had a side weakened by the loss of several players in the tragic Munich air crash, and limped out in the group stages.

Chile, in South America, was the venue for the 1962 competition. England arrived full of hope and played well to beat Argentina and qualify for the quarter-finals. They then met Brazil, and although they played well, finally lost out 3-1 to the eventual cup winners.

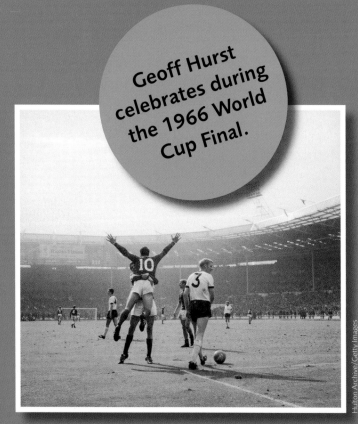

Geoff Hurst celebrates during the 1966 World Cup Final.

8

You can read more about England's 4-2 win over West Germany in the Final on page 86.

England captain Bobby Moore with the World Cup in 1966.

In 1966 the World Cup came to England and that summer there was a fantastic festival of football across the whole country! England made it through to a quarter-final with Argentina which they won 1-0, before taking on Portugal in the semi-final. It turned out to be one of the best games of the tournament. England were two up before the famous Portuguese player Eusebio pulled one back with a penalty. The last ten minutes were frantic but England held on.

Expectations were high in Mexico for the 1970 tournament. After all, England were defending champions! England were drawn in the same group as Brazil but managed to scrape through and then took on their great rivals West Germany in a quarter-final. But despite leading 2-0 they let the lead slip and went out 3-2 in extra time.

Then came a very bleak 12 years as England failed to qualify for the finals in 1974 and 1978. England had some great players at the time such as Kevin Keegan, Tony Currie and Alan Hudson, but they just couldn't gel together as a team.

Geoff Hurst again, this time in action against Romania at the 1970 World Cup.

England returned to the world stage in Spain in 1982 but although they never lost a game – and only conceded one goal – their failure to score cost them dear. They went out at the second round stage, just before the semi-finals.

England's Trevor Francis races Marius Tresor of France to the ball during the 1982 tournament.

World Cup

England were also goal shy at the 1986 finals in Mexico. And they risked early elimination again until Gary Lineker's hat-trick against Poland. He scored two more against Paraguay to see England through to the quarters, where they came up against a Maradona-inspired Argentina, and went out 2-1.

Gary Lineker scores against Paraguay at the famous Azteca Stadium in 1986.

At Italia 90 England did far better than anyone expected. Coming through a tricky group, they saw off Belgium in the second round and Cameroon in the quarters before going out to West Germany on penalties in the semi-final. They finally finished fourth, losing a 3rd place play-off game with hosts Italy 2-1.

Paul Scholes (above) scored once as England beat Tunisia 2-0 in a group game at France 1998.

In 1994 there was more disappointment when England missed out on taking part in the first World Cup to be held in the USA.

Paul Gascoigne had a great World Cup for England at Italia 90.

World Cup

In 1998 they crossed the English Channel to France, and again it was penalties that ended their hopes. Having scraped through to the second round they came up against Argentina and despite leading 2-1, they were eliminated after another dreaded shoot-out.

The 2002 Finals were the first to be held in Asia, with South Korea and Japan the joint hosts. Again England made it through the opening rounds but this time came up against the mighty Brazil in the quarters, losing 2-1.

Wayne Rooney bursts through the Swedish defence at the 2006 World Cup.

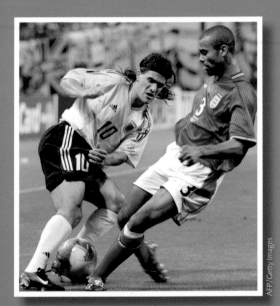

Argentinian midfielder Ariel Ortega and England's Ashley Cole fight for the ball during their World Cup clash in 2002.

The last World Cup, in 2006, was held in Germany, and to be honest, England never really got going. They eased through a pretty easy group but once again went out on penalties, this time to Portugal.

And so to 2010, when the World Cup arrives in Africa for the first time, with South Africa the host. Can't wait!

For the record

England at the World Cup

1930 – didn't enter	Winners: Uruguay
1934 – didn't enter	Winners: Italy
1938 – didn't enter	Winners: Italy
1950 – out at group stage	Winners: Uruguay
1954 – quarter-finals	Winners: West Germany
1958 – out at group stage	Winners: Brazil
1962 – quarter-finals	Winners: Brazil
1966 – winners	
1970 – quarter-finals	Winners: Brazil
1974 – did not qualify	Winners: West Germany
1978 – did not qualify	Winners: Argentina
1982 – second round	Winners: Italy
1986 – quarter-finals	Winners: Argentina
1990 – fourth	Winners: West Germany
1994 – did not qualify	Winners: Brazil
1998 – second round	Winners: France
2002 – quarter-finals	Winners: Brazil
2006 – quarter-finals	Winners: Italy

European Championship

England have always performed pretty well in the World Cup but they've never really lived up to their potential in the European Championship.

Played every four years, the goal is to find the best footballing country in Europe.

England opted out of the first tournament and perhaps wished they'd given the second competition a wide berth too, with France knocking them out 6-3 over two matches in 1964.

In 1968, they got through to the semi-finals, before losing to Yugoslavia. However they did beat the Soviet Union in a play-off for third place, which was to prove their best ever finish.

Michael Owen scores against Portugal in 2004 – but it wasn't enough.

AFP/Getty Images

Owen Hargreaves in action against Switzerland in a group match during Euro 2004.

Getty Images Sport/Getty Images

England cruised through qualifying in 1972, dropping just one point. But they came up against West Germany in the quarter-final. Having lost 3-1 at Wembley, the 0-0 draw in Berlin was no use to them, and out they went.

In 1976 they failed to qualify but were unbeaten in the run up to the 1980 finals, which were held in just one country, Italy, for the first time. But England flopped and didn't make it through the group stage.

They missed out again in 1984, finishing second in their qualifying group to Denmark, but their tails were up again in 1988 after they edged into the finals in West Germany.

But then it all went wrong! They finished bottom of their group, with just one point and two goal from three games.

In 1996 England hosted the tournament and the team played some of their best football since the 1966 World Cup. Alan Shearer was scoring goals for fun, and Paul Gascoigne was in excellent form. Scotland and Spain were beaten along the way to a semi-final encounter with Germany, where England lost a nail-biting penalty shoot-out (see page 88).

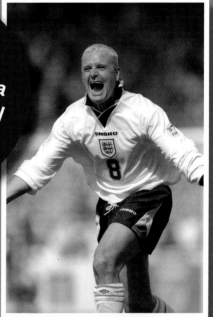

Gazza celebrates after scoring a great individual goal against Scotland at Euro 96.

Getty Images Sport/Getty Images

Even a 1-0 win against Germany wasn't enough to see England through at Euro 2000. Alan Shearer was the scorer.

Bongarts/Getty Images

In 2000, despite a great start – England were two up against Portugal after just 18 minutes in their opening game – and were out in the first round.

And it was Portugal that did it to England again in 2004, beating them on penalties in the thrilling quarter-finals (see page 91).

In 2008 Austria and Switzerland will share the finals and England will be hoping to put an end to their European Championship jinx once and for all!

For the record

England in the European Championship

1960 – did not enter	Winner: Soviet Union (Russia)
1964 – out in first round	Winner: Spain
1968 – third	Winner: Italy
1972 – quarter-finals	Winner: West Germany
1976 – did not qualify	Winner: Czechoslovakia
1980 – out at group stage	Winner: West Germany
1984 – did not qualify	Winner: France
1988 – out at group stage	Winner: Holland
1992 – out at group stage	Winner: Denmark
1996 – semi-finals	Winner: Germany
2000 – out at group stage	Winner: France
2004 – quarter-final	Winner: Greece

Rivals - Argentina

Over 90 minutes at least, England have a very good record against Argentina. But over the years there are two games in particular that stand out – unfortunately England lost them both!

After a couple of friendlies, the first competitive meeting came in 1962, when England ran out 3-1 winners in a World Cup group game.

Then came a momentous clash in the quarter-final of the 1966 World Cup. The Argentina skipper Antonio Rattin became the first ever player to be sent off in an England home game. The South Americans never really recovered, with England winning 1-0 in the end.

But it was to be another World Cup quarter-final twenty years later, this time at the Azteca Stadium in Mexico City, where the rivalry hit boiling point.

The tragic end to World Cup dreams by the hand of Maradona.

Diego Maradona and The Hand of God.

Bongarts/Getty Images

England had done well to get this far, while Argentina were coasting thanks largely to one man, a footballing genius by the name of Diego Maradona. The first half was goalless and England were holding their own. Then Maradona challenged the England keeper Peter Shilton for a high ball in the box. And suddenly the ball was in the net.

'Hand ball!' protested the England players. 'Goal,' said the ref. Maradona went wild although he would later describe it as the 'Hand of God' goal – in other words admitting he had punched the ball in.

But minutes later the other Maradona appeared – Maradona the magician, as he dribbled his way past half the England team to slot the ball home. Gary Lineker scored late on but England were out.

Fast forward 12 years to France and a World Cup second round clash. This time Argentina took the lead, scoring a penalty in the first few minutes. But England were soon level with a goal of their own - Alan Shearer scored from the penalty spot after five minutes.

Cue Michael Owen. Picking the ball up on the halfway line he ran, and ran and ran before unleashing a shot that flew past the keeper. But by half-time Argentina had equalised once more.

Then disaster struck. Just two minutes into the second period and David Beckham was sent off. England held on for penalties, but their record in shoot-outs was woeful. And sadly nothing changed that night as they lost 4-3 on penalties.

The Boy Wonder Michael Owen during the 1988 World Cup clash.

But revenge, so the saying goes, is sweet and the two sides met once more in a group match at Japan's Sapporo Dome at the 2002 World Cup. And this time they did score a penalty, Beckham coverting to see England home 1-0.

Get in there! Beckham celebrates after scoring in the 2002 World Cup group game.

For the record

England v Argentina

Played	14
Won	6
Drawn	6
Lost	2
Goals for	21
Goals against	15

Amazing fact:

The second time the two teams met, in May 1953, goes down in history as only one of the two times an England game has ever been abandoned. The reason – torrential Argentine rain.

Even the last time they met, in a friendly in 2005, proved to be eventful. With just three minutes left Argentina looked to be home and dry at 2-1 up. But they hadn't reckoned on Michael Owen again, who popped up with two late goals to seal a remarkable 3-2 win.

Rivals - Brazil

England's games against the mighty Brazil have actually been few and far between. But when the Three Lions do come up against the Boys from Brazil, there's never a dull moment!

The first big encounter came during the 1958 World Cup Finals in Sweden when they played out the first 0-0 draw in World Cup history!

Playing Brazil in 1958 they played out the first 0-0 draw in World Cup history!

England's Don Howe (white shirt) during the goalless draw in Sweden.

They met again four years later in the quarter-finals of the 1962 World Cup when Brazil were convincing 3-1 winners. The match is best remembered for a dog running on the pitch and the England striker Jimmy Greaves going down on all fours to try and encourage it to leave!

In 1970 they were drawn in the same group during the Mexico World Cup. And this time the memorable moment was an incredible save by the great English keeper Gordon Banks.

The great Gordon Banks denies the legendary Pele.

Pele, probably the most famous footballer ever, sent a powerful header towards goal. And he was already starting to celebrate his 'goal' when, in a flash, Banks dived to his right and just managed to tip the ball round the post. Although England played well, they finally lost 1-0.

Pele and England captain Bobby Moore swap shirts.

16

A dozen friendlies followed until the sides met at the quarter-final stage again, this time in Japan at the 2002 World Cup. And it turned out to be another cracker!

England scored first, with Michael Owen's pace opening up the Brazilian defence, before he confidently chipped the ball over the keeper. But Brazil equalised on the stroke of half-time.

Then, after just five minutes of the second half, Ronaldinho sent a high, hopeful free kick into the box. But it caught England keeper David Seaman off guard. He back-pedalled furiously but couldn't stop it dropping in under the bar at the far post.

England's Tony Currie and Brazilian great Zico during a 1-1 draw at Wembley in 1978.

David Beckham and Roberto Carlos tussle for the ball in 2002.

For the record

England v Brazil

Played	21
Won	3
Drawn	8
Lost	10
Goals for	18
Goals against	29

Amazing fact:

A team has only scored more than two goals in four of the 21 games between the two countries.

But the twists kept on coming and just eight minutes later the goalscorer was harshly sent off, forcing Brazil to play out the final half an hour with just ten men. But try as they might, England couldn't get back on level terms.

In all, England have only beaten Brazil three times. But there's always an intense rivalry between the countries. After all, England 'invented' the modern game, while the Brazilians have shown us all how to play it!

Rivals - France

Brave keeping from England's Frank Swift during the 1947 international.

There's always been a healthy rivalry between England and France, whether at football, rugby, or even tiddlywinks!

To start with, the football matches were one-sided affairs and it was England not France who were magnifique!

England won 11 of the first 12 games, including a 6-0 win in France and a 3-0 win at Arsenal's old Highbury Ground in 1947.

The first major clash came in the European Nations Cup (we now know it as the European Championship). After a 1-1 draw at Wembley, England went to Paris but were soundly thrashed 5-2.

They met again during the 1966 World Cup and this time it was England's turn to celebrate, with a 2-0 win.

England full-back Ray Wilson slides in at Wembley in 1966.

England's Paul Mariner, who set up Robson for his historic goal.

The teams avoided each other throughout the 1970s but met again during the 1982 World Cup in Spain. And what a welcome England gave France, with Bryan Robson scoring after just 27 seconds! England finally won 3-1, which was no mean achievement against a French team that would go on to become one of the best teams in the world.

There's not much to say about the bore draw at the 1992 European Championship in Sweden, so we'll move on to the most recent match between the two sides. Although it's one that most England fans will want to forget!

Portugal 2004 and England faced France, the defending European Champions. Frank Lampard had headed England into the lead after 38 minutes and although David Beckham later missed a penalty, England were holding on. And as the 90 minutes were up, they looked set for a famous victory.

> Frank Lampard header gives England the lead in 2004.

England's David Platt and France's Didier Deschamps just about manage to stay awake during their 1992 game in Malmo.

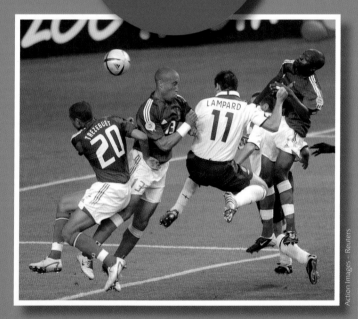

But they hadn't reckoned on Zinedine Zidane. First he curled a free kick past David James in the England goal to make it 1-1. Then, in what was the last attack of the match, James fouled Thierry Henry in the box – penalty.

Cool as you like, up stepped Zidane again, calmly slotting the ball home and giving France an unbelievable extra time victory!

For the record

England v France

Played	26
Won	16
Drawn	4
Lost	6
Goals for	65
Goals against	32

Amazing fact:

Masek scored after 15 seconds in Czechoslovakia V Mexico in 1962. This was the quickest goal in World Cup history until Hakan Sukur scored after just 11 seconds for Turkey in 2002.

Rivals - Germany

From World Cup Finals to nail-biting penalty shoot-outs, there's no getting away from it – England and Germany are the greatest rivals in world football.

(Just for the record, Germany was known as West Germany between 1954-1990. But we'll just keep it as plain old Germany for now. There was an East Germany as well but don't worry too much about that!)

It all began with a 3-3 draw in May 1930 but it wasn't until England won the 1966 World Cup Final 4-2 (see page 86) that the rivalry really started to heat up.

A moment of sheer joy for Gary Lineker as he equalises against the Germans in 1990.

England's Colin Bell in action against Germany during the 1970 World Cup clash.

Germany took their revenge four years later in the heat of Mexico, sending England crashing out of the World Cup at the quarter-final stage, 3-2. Incredibly England had been 2-0 up as well. Many people say it took England well over ten years to recover from the shock! What is true is that they failed to even qualify for the next two finals.

There was more English pain two years later when Germany won 3-1 at Wembley to dump England out of the European Championship. A 0-0 draw in the 1982 World Cup was enough to eliminate England from yet another competition, so the players who lined up to face Germany in the semi-final of Italia 1990 can be forgiven for being a little bit worried!

England fell behind on the hour mark but equalised through Gary Lineker with ten minutes to go. There were no more goals, so the game went to extra time. But still the deadlock wasn't broken so the game went to penalties.

With England 4-3 down, Chris Waddle had to score England's fourth kick. Unfortunately, so the joke goes, the ball is still orbiting the moon today! Poor Chris blazed it miles over the bar and England were knocked out by the Germans yet again.

Michael Owen and Germany's Thomas Linke during the last game at Wembley.

In 1996 they met again, this time in the semi-final of the European Championship (see page 88). But once again England's penalty jinx struck.

Alan Shearer scored the only goal in a 1-0 win in a group game at Euro 2000 and then came two qualifying games for the 2002 World Cup.

The first saw Germany win 1-0 in the last ever international game at Wembley. It also proved to be Kevin Keegan's last game in charge. But then came Munich 2001. It's a match no England fan will ever forget. And you can read more about that one on page 90.

And so the rivalry goes on and England just about have the upper hand at the moment – as long as the game doesn't go to penalties that is!

Alan Shearer scored the only goal in a 1-0 win in a group game at Euro 2000.

For the record

England v Germany

Played	25
Won	11
Drawn	5
Lost	10
Goals for	44
Goals against	31

Amazing fact:
England played East Germany four times in friendlies, winning three and drawing once.

Peter Crouch playing for England against Spain in February 2007

Play the Game

ENGLAND

Next up is a great selection of games, puzzles and quizzes that will test your footballing knowledge to the full. There's also the chance to design your very own England kit!

Activities

True or false?

1. England play in yellow shirts and pink shorts.

2. Ronaldo is a goalkeeper.

3. A football match lasts 90 minutes.

4. The first World Cup was held in Italy.

5. Brazil have won the World Cup four times.

Ground control

Can you solve the clues to find the name of a famous Premiership football ground? You have to work out which letter is the answer to each clue. The first word of the answer has 3 letters, the second 8.

1.   My first is in corner but not in ball

2.   My second is in flag but not in net

3.   My third is in defence but not in goal

4.   My fourth is in trophy but not in medal

5.   My fifth is in ref but not in pitch

6.   My sixth is in Arsenal but not in Everton

7.   My seventh is in first but not in second

8.   My eighth is in Fulham but not in Ipswich

9.   My ninth is in oval but not in an egg

10.   My tenth is in Ryan but never in Giggs

11.   My eleventh is in dummy but not in a trick

Word search

The World Cup is held every four years. Here are some of the countries it's been held in. Can you find them all in the grid below?

Argentina
Brazil
Chile
England
France
Italy
Mexico

Spain
Sweden
Switzerland
Uruguay
USA
Germany

```
S   W   I   T       Z       E       R       L       A       N       D       P
E   R   I   I       Q       W       E       L       R       O       P       C
S   T   T   I   S   K   H   G   L   K   G   W   E   M
N   Y   A   I   S   C   H   I   L   U   E   R   T   E
E   U   L   S   J   P   H   H   J   J   N   Y   U   X
D   I   Y   R   P   H   Y   N   J   I   O   D   I
E   G   S   V   M   A   N   Y   N   T   O   N   C
W   C   E   G   U   G   I   T   I   O   A   I
S   C   C   G   S   G   R   Y   N   O   L   C
D   F   Y   Z   A   D   F   N   A   P   G   O
B   R   U   H   I   L   F   B   D   L   N   T
U   R   L       G   F   R   V   X   L   E   Y
                                A   N   C   U
```

Activities

Design a kit

As you know, England play in white shirts with navy blue shorts and white socks. Add in the Three Lions on the crest and you've got one of the most famous football kits in the world.

But for a change, why not have a go at designing your own England kit. Simply photocopy these pages and away you go. Perhaps you could even have a competition with your friends at school and ask your teacher to choose the best one!

Guess who?

Can you guess who's hiding in these pictures?

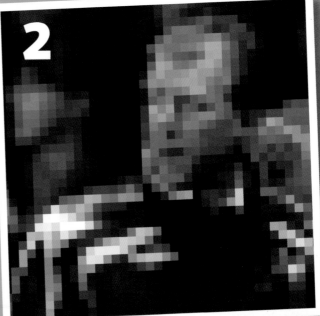

Activities

A gap in the defence!

Using the words below, fill in the gaps to complete the names of some of the Premiership's most famous footballers.

Words

JAM
ART
BALL
BELL
LAMP

OUCH
DOWN
BEAT
BIN
SICK

1.   _ _ _ _ A C K (Chelsea)

2.   R O _ _ _ S O N (Spurs)

3.   _ _ _ _ A M Y (Liverpool)

4.   R O _ _ _ _ Y (Arsenal)

5.   _ _ _ _ A R D (Chelsea)

6.   _ _ _ _ T I E (Everton)

7.   C R _ _ _ _ (Liverpool)

8.   B _ _ _ O N (Manchester City)

9.   _ _ _ _ I N G (Middlesbrough)

10.   _ _ _ E S (Portsmouth)

What's in a name?

Can you unscramble the letters to find the names of some famous England players? As a clue, we've put the team they play for in brackets next to them.

1. NO HERRY JT   (Chelsea)

2. CROP CUT HERE   (Liverpool)

3. RAY NONE WE YO   (Man Utd)

4. DANGER ERR VEST   (Liverpool)

5. CARD AM RICH HIS   (Man City)

Spot the difference

Can you find 6 differences between these two pictures?

AFP/Getty Images

AFP/Getty Images

Activities

Getty Images Sport/Getty Images

Code breaker

The England manager has heard that there are spies trying to find out who he's going to pick to play in a crucial qualifying game. To confuse them he's come up with a cunning plan!

Not only has he swapped the letters in their name for a special sign but he's also written them on the sheet in the wrong position. Can you find out who he's picked to play in the big match?

1.
2.
3.
4.
5.
6.
7.
8.
9.
10.
11.

Key

A - ✌ B - 🖐 C - 👍 D - 👎 E - ☞ F - ☞

G - ☝ H - 👆 I - 🖐 J - ☺ K - 😐 L - ☹

M - 💣 N - ☠ O - ⚑ P - ⚐ Q - ✈ R - ☼

S - ♦ T - ❄ U - ✝ V - ✟ W - ⚚ X - ✠

Y - ✡ Z - ☪

Activities

Fantastic Football

Look at the photo of this great action shot. Then copy the image, square by square, into the larger grid below.

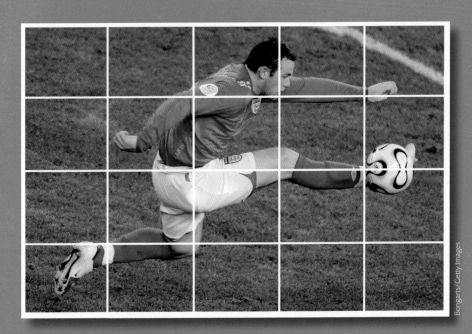

Bongarts/Getty Images

31

Activities

Player search

Can you find these England players hidden in the grid below?

TERRY
GERRARD
DEFOE
ROONEY
PARKER
COLE
CROUCH
KIRKLAND
OWEN
LAMPARD

```
R  E  C  L  C  N  D  P
O  E  R  R  O  P  C  E
O  H  O  K  L  W  E  M
N  P  U  L  E  R  E  E
E  A  C  N  Y  U  X  N
Y  R  H  T  O  D  I  P
A  K  D  E  F  O  E  L
G  E  R  R  A  L  D  O
R  R  A  R  G  T  R  F
F  O  D  Y  P  T  S  U
V  L  A  M  L  A  R  D
K  I  R  K  M  A  N  D
```

Action Images - Reuters

Football funnies

What have a bad goalkeeper and Dracula got in common?

They both hate crosses!

Why did the footballer take an early bath?

Because he was caught playing dirty!

Why did the manager flood the pitch?

Because he wanted to bring on his sub!

Why did the footballer think he was a chicken?

Because the referee called 'foul'!

Why did the defender bring a broom onto the pitch?

Because he was a sweeper!

Why do goalkeepers have a bath before bedtime?

To keep clean sheets!

Mixed up

Unjumble the letters below to find five things you'd find on a football pitch.

WOT STEAM	_ _ _ / _ _ _ _ _
CHAMT LABL	_ _ _ _ _ / _ _ _ _
STOP GO LAS	_ _ _ _ _ _ _ _
FER ERE E	_ _ _ _ _ _ _
HIT SLEW	_ _ _ _ _ _

Activities

Footy crossword

Can you answer all the clues below to solve the crossword?

Across

3. Which London football team does England skipper, John Terry, play for?

4. Name the member of the England first team who plays for the German club side Bayern Munich.

6. England's Under-21 team played the first game at which new stadium in March 2007?

8. What surname do the two brothers on the England squad share?

10. What month of 2006 was Steve McClaren confirmed as the new England manager?

11. Which London club side did England defender Ashley Cole play for before moving to Chelsea in 2006?

Down

1. Which South American team did England play their first game against in the 2006 World Cup Finals?

2. What is the name of the England assistant coach?

5. Which member of the England team, who also plays for Liverpool FC, was awarded an MBE in March 2007?

7. What is the surname of the England striker who plays for Manchester United FC?

ENGLAND

Activities

Spot the ball
OK, where's the ball in this picture?

1
2
3
4
5

A B C D E F

AFP/Getty Images

Wayne Rooney attacking hard against Israel in March 2007

True or false?

1. False
2. False – he's a winger
3. True
4. False – it was Uruguay
5. False – it's five

Ground control

Old Trafford

Word Search

S	W	I	T	Z	E	R	L	A	N	D	P
E	R	T	I	Q	W	E	L	R	O	P	C
S	T	A	I	K	H	G	K	G	W	E	M
N	Y	L	S	S	C	H	I	L	E	T	E
E	U	Y	S	P	H	U	O	N	R	U	X
D	I	S	J	P	Y	Y	Y	T	Y	D	I
E	W	G	E	R	M	A	N	Y	O	N	C
W	C	C	V	U	G	I	T	O	A	L	O
S	C	Y	G	S	G	R	N	P	L	G	T
D	F	U	G	A	D	F	B	D	L	N	T
B	R	A	Z	I	L	F	V	X	N	E	Y
U	R	L	H	G	F	R	A	N	C	E	U

Guess who?

1. Frank Lampard
2. Steve McClaren
3. Owen Hargreaves
4. Michael Owen

A gap in the defence!

BALLACK	(Chelsea)
ROBINSON	(Spurs)
BELLAMY	(Liverpool)
ROSICKY	(Arsenal)
LAMPARD	(Chelsea)
BEATTIE	(Everton)
CROUCH	(Liverpool)
BARTON	(Manchester City)
DOWNING	(Middlesbrough)
JAMES	(Portsmouth)

What's in a name?

1. JOHN TERRY
2. PETER CROUCH
3. WAYNE ROONEY
4. STEVEN GERRARD
5. MICAH RICHARDS

Spot the difference

Activities - Answers

Code breaker

1. Terry
2. Lampard
3. Robinson
4. Ferdinand
5. Barton
6. Rooney
7. Owen
8. Lennon
9. Neville
10. Gerrard
11. Cole

Player search

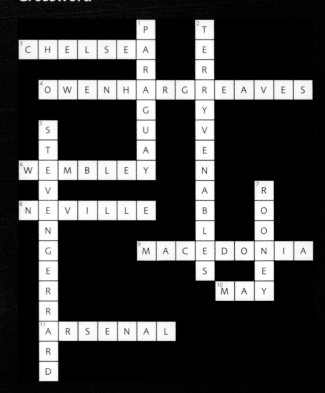

Mixed up

1. TWO TEAMS
2. MATCH BALL
3. GOALPOSTS
4. REFEREE
5. WHISTLE

Crossword

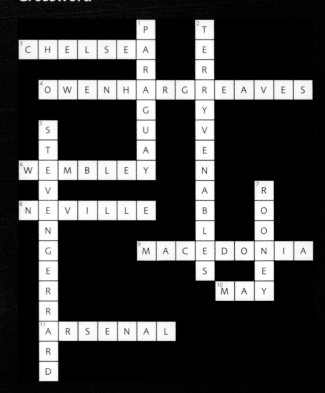

Spot the ball

AFP/Getty Images

Profiles

Do you know which England player was filmed playing keepie-uppie for a TV advert? Or who's England's youngest ever goalscorer? Read on for the low-down on England's top international stars.

Team Profile

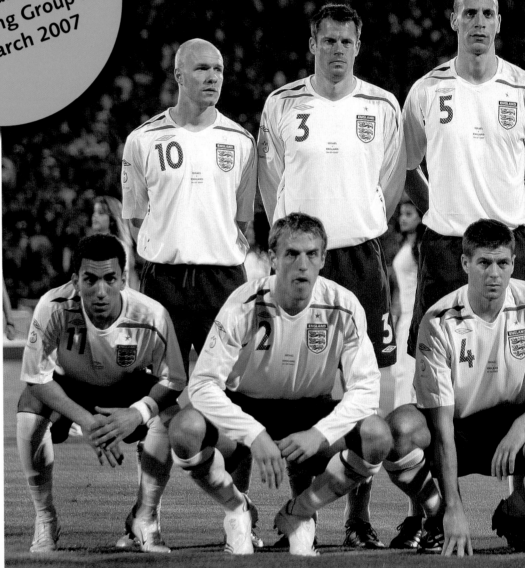

Group line-up
Israel v England
UEFA Euro 2008
Qualifying Group E
24 March 2007

(front row: left-right)

Aaron Lennon, Philip Neville, Steven Gerrard, Owen Hargreaves and Wayne Rooney

England (back row: left-right)

Andrew Johnson, Jamie Carragher, Rio Ferdinand, John Terry, Paul Robinson and Frank Lampard

Action Images – Reuters

Peter Crouch

Born: 30.01.81, Macclesfield

Club side: Liverpool FC

Position: Centre-forward

Debut: v Colombia, 31.05.05

Caps: 17

You won't be surprised to know that at 2.01m (6ft 7in), Crouchy is the tallest man ever to play for England. He already looks set to become one of our greatest goal scorers too; in 2006 he became the first Englishman to score ten goals in one calendar year. For such a big lad he's also got great ball control and he's smashed home some pretty acrobatic goals.

In fact there's little doubt that Crouchy has already become something of a cult hero. And who'll ever forget the footage of him doing his famous robot dance in front of Prince William at a training session before the last World Cup!

Action Images – Reuters

Jermain Defoe

Born: 07.10.82, London

Club side: Tottenham Hotspur FC

Position: Forward

Debut: v Sweden, 31.03.04

Caps: 24

Renowned for his blistering pace and fierce shot, Jermain is one of England's brightest prospects. Despite winning 23 caps at U21 level (the sixth highest ever) he didn't make it to the last World Cup. However, he looks set to be a part of Steve McClaren's plans, especially if he carries on scoring so regularly for Spurs.

Football is in his blood, too. "I grew up in East London and that's all I used to do, playing five-a-side with my mates," he says. "That's all I wanted to do when I was younger, even when I was in school. It was hard for me to concentrate when I was in school, because I couldn't wait until the bell so I could go out and play football."

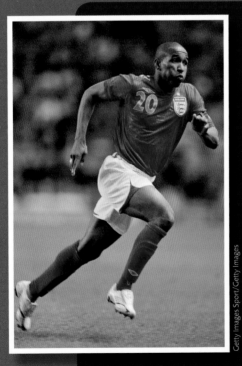

Getty Images Sport/ Getty Images

ENGLAND

Michael Owen

Born: 14.12.79, Chester
Club side: Newcastle United FC
Position: Forward
Debut: v Chile, 11.02.98
Caps: 80

After scoring over 100 goals for Liverpool, Michael was tempted to try his luck with Real Madrid. Unfortunately it didn't work out and despite the temptation to return to Anfield, he joined Newcastle United in 2005.

Michael burst on to the international scene at the 1998 World Cup with a fantastic individual goal against Argentina. He's been steadily working his way up England's all-time goal scorer chart ever since. Probably his most famous game for England came in the startling 5-1 demolition of Germany in 2001, when he notched a hat-trick.

A quick-thinking striker who's lethal in the box, he's sadly been hit by a string of injuries in recent years, including a horrible twisted knee in the last World Cup. But when he's fit, you just know he's one of the first names the manager puts on the team sheet.

Wayne Rooney

Born: 24.10.85, Liverpool

Club side: Manchester United FC

Position: Forward

Debut: v Australia, 12.02.03

Caps: 38

Wayne started grabbing the headlines as a 16-year-old at Everton and it wasn't long before Rooneymania had taken hold! His performances for the Blues attracted the attention of a certain Sir Alex Ferguson, who got out his cheque book (well, Manchester United's at least!) and paid a colossal £20 million to bring Wayne to Old Trafford.

He now looks set to become one of England's greatest ever players. Seriously skillful and incredibly strong, he can dribble, shoot and head the ball like a bullet. England's second youngest debutant and youngest ever goal scorer, over the next ten years expect plenty more international records to be heading his way!

Michael Carrick

Born: 28.07.81, Wallsend
Club side: Manchester United FC
Position: Midfield
Debut: v Mexico, 25.05.01
Caps: 12

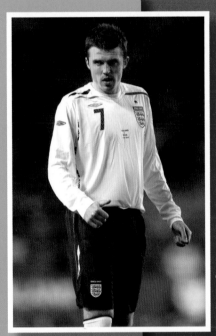

Action Images – Reuters

Michael learned his football at the same boys club, Wallsend, that's produced a whole team of England internationals, including true greats like Alan Shearer and Peter Beardsley. So you could say he had a good start in life!

Despite being brought up in the North East, Michael decided to seek his fortune in London. He made his name at West Ham United, before moving on to Spurs, and then back up north to Manchester United. He's become an important part of the England set-up – a midfield lynch pin who can tackle to break up attacks and pass the ball brilliantly. He also knows when to hold on to the ball and the importance of keeping possession to slow the game down.

Joe Cole

Getty Images Sport/Getty Images

Born: 08.11.81, London
Club side: Chelsea FC
Position: Right midfield/wing
Debut: v Mexico, 25.05.01
Caps: 38

Joe's a wonderfully gifted, attacking player who's become a vital part of the England team. Like England colleagues Frank Lampard and Rio Ferdinand, Joe's another product of the successful West Ham youth academy.

But while no one ever doubted his skill and talent, there were question marks about whether he was a real team player. But under Chelsea boss Jose Mourinho he's developed into a world-class footballer. He scores great goals too, including a scorching volley against Sweden in the last World Cup that was one of the strikes of the tournament.

As he says, "There are a lot of negative aspects to the football world, but I like to think I'm quite a good role model... I like to enjoy my football without the glitz and the glamour. I do my best to stay level-headed and behave properly." Good for Joe.

Kieron Dyer

Born: 29.12.78, Ipswich
Club side: Newcastle United FC
Position: Left midfield
Debut: v Luxembourg, 04.09.99
Caps: 30

Kieron first caught the eye at Ipswich Town in the mid-1990s, before moving on to Newcastle United in 1999. He's now made over 250 appearances for the Magpies.

Were it not for a string of niggling injuries, Kieron would surely have collected far more England caps by now. A quick, combative player, who's very hard to shake off the ball, he's got a great turn of speed that can take him past most defenders. That said, he's still not scored for the senior team yet.

But while he may be 'Speedy Gonzalez' on the pitch, off it he likes to take life nice and slow. In fact he quite often has a two-and-a-half hour nap after training!

Steven Gerrard

Born: 30.05.80, Liverpool
Club side: Liverpool FC
Position: Midfield
Debut: v Ukraine, 31.05.00
Caps: 55

Steven Gerrard is a manager's dream! Although his favoured position is central midfield, he can play just about anywhere from out on the wing, to just behind the centre-forward. He can also sit in front of the back four or surge forward through the middle of the park. In fact he's even slotted in at right-back! Oh, and did I mention those wonderful goals he loves scoring...

He's a bit of a lucky omen too, and had played 22 times for England before he tasted defeat.

He was awarded an MBE in the New Year's Honours list – which basically means he gets to meet the Queen at Buckingham Palace! Mind you, he's quite used to winning awards and his mantelpiece must be groaning under the weight as he's also won the PFA Young Player of the Year, PFA Player of the Year, European Midfielder of the Year, Premier League Most Valuable Player (twice) and UEFA Most Valuable Player.

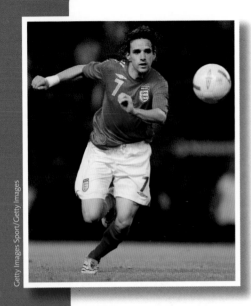

Getty Images Sport/Getty Images

Owen Hargreaves

Born: 20.01.81, Canada

Club side: Bayern Munich (Germany)

Position: Midfield

Debut: v Holland, 15.08.01

Caps: 39

Born in Canada and brought up in Germany, Owen could have played for any of four countries but chose England and made his U21 debut in 2000. He's a player who's fast and supremely fit, a real midfield dynamo who does the simple things well.

No one in the squad was the least bit surprised when fans voted Owen as England's player of the 2006 World Cup. He'd put in two superb performances against both Sweden and Portugal and won over the supporters who at first had wanted a more creative player in the squad.

Frank Lampard

Born: 20.06.78, Romford

Club side: Chelsea

Position: Central midfield

Debut: v Belgium, 10.10.99

Caps: 53

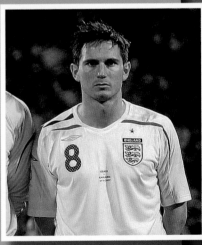

Action Images – Reuters

Frank has matured into one of the best midfielders in the world. A real box to box player, he can boss games from the centre of the park. He's also got a powerful shot, and has struck several superb goals from well outside the penalty area.

Super fit too, he holds the record for playing in the Premiership more times in a row than any other player. He managed an incredible 160 games on the trot!

And as his boss Jose Mourinho says, "He plays every day, he plays every game. Cold, hot, rain, snow, against tough opponents, against soft opponents, at home, away from home and with somebody trying to mark him man to man."

Voted Official England Player of the Year by the fans in 2004 and 2005, his dad, Frank Senior, also played for England.

ENGLAND

Aaron Lennon

Born: 16.04.87, Leeds

Club side: Tottenham Hotspur FC

Position: Winger

Debut: v Jamaica, 03.06.06

Caps: 9

England may not have enjoyed the best of times at the last World Cup in Germany, but if there was one bright light it was in the form of Aaron Lennon. When he came on as a substitute his speed terrorised tiring defenders, who were never sure exactly where this tricky little winger would twist and turn next!

In August 2003, Aaron became the youngest player in Premiership history when he came off the bench for his former club Leeds United against Spurs. He was aged just 16 years and 129 days. In 2005 he joined Spurs but while he may have become a firm favourite with the fans at White Hart Lane, he'll always have a soft spot for their great London rivals, Chelsea, a club he started supporting as a boy.

Phil Neville

Born: 21.01.77, Bury

Club side: Everton FC

Position: Midfield

Debut: v China, 23.05.96

Caps: 56

Phil enjoyed over ten years of success at Manchester United before moving on to Everton in 2005. 'Mr Versatile' can play in defence or midfield, and he's one of those players that teammates come to rely on.

As Phil explains, he could also have played cricket at the highest level but chose football instead. "In my opinion, I was better at cricket but United offered me a YTS (Youth Training Scheme) apprenticeship and there was nothing on offer from cricket. So I gave it up, concentrated on my schoolwork as well as I could and then joined United when the time came." By the way, one of his teammates at Lancashire was a certain Andrew Flintoff. Perhaps you've heard of him!

47

Player Profiles

Shaun Wright-Phillips

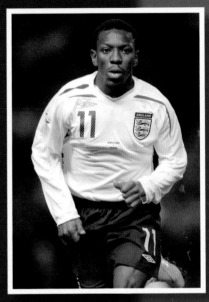

Born: 25.10.81, London

Club side: Chelsea FC

Position: Winger

Debut: v Ukraine, 18.08.04

Caps: 12

With blistering pace, a thunderous shot and a host of tricks up his sleeve, SWP, as he's known, looks set for a bright future in an England shirt.

He was actually released by Nottingham Forest as a 15-year-old because they thought he was too small (true, he is only 1.68 m (5 ft 6 in)) but was snapped up by Manchester City, where he developed into one of the Premiership's most exciting players.

He took the hard decision to move south and join Chelsea in 2005 for an estimated £21 million. In case you didn't know, he was adopted as a kid by Arsenal great – and TV pundit – Ian Wright. But he's already got one up on Dad by scoring on his England debut, something Ian didn't manage.

Action Images – Reuters

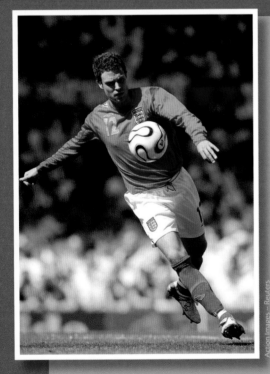

Action Images – Reuters

Wayne Bridge

Born: 05.08.80, Southampton

Club side: Chelsea FC

Position: Left-back

Debut: v Holland, 13.02.02

Caps: 24

Wayne's another England defender who's more than happy to gallop forward with the ball at his feet and one eye on goal! He began his career at Southampton before packing his bags and moving to Chelsea. In fact, he became one of the first signings made by the club's rather rich new owner, Roman Abramovich.

He's played in the last two World Cup Finals, although he often finds himself starting on the bench for both club and country thanks to the form of his friend Ashley Cole! Because of this he's attracted a lot of interest from other Premiership clubs but now he's signed a deal with Chelsea, he looks set to keep fighting for a regular first team place at Stamford Bridge.

ENGLAND

Jamie Carragher

Born: 28.01.78, Liverpool
Club side: Liverpool FC
Position: Centre-back
Debut: v Hungary, 28.04.99
Caps: 33

Strong and committed, 'Carra' is unlucky to have such strong competition for a regular place in England's starting line-up. After a record-breaking haul of caps for the U21s, he's become a versatile player who can also play at full-back and perform a holding role in midfield. He also put in several solid performances at the last World Cup.

He's one of the most popular players at Anfield and was the highest placed defender in a recent poll of the fans' favourites. He finished seventh. He's also been honoured by the local people of Sefton, where he lives, as a great role model for the young people. All in all, a pretty good bloke!

Ashley Cole

Born: 20.12.80, London
Club side: Chelsea FC
Position: Left-back
Debut: v Albania, 28.03.01
Caps: 58

If ever a player loved the big occasion, it's Ashley! He's been an England regular since 2001, thanks to an electric turn of pace and a natural attacking ability. However, although he loves to get forward, he's yet to score an international goal!

Ashley made his name with Arsenal, where he made well over 200 appearances, but in 2006 he moved across London to Chelsea. In fact the summer of 2006 was a busy time for Ashley, because no sooner was he back from the World Cup, he was walking down the aisle and getting married to Cheryl Tweedy, singer with top popsters Girls Aloud.

Player Profiles

Rio Ferdinand

Born: 07.11.78, London

Club side: Manchester United FC

Position: Centre-back

Debut: v Cameroon, 15.11.97

Caps: 59

A classy defender who's a tenacious tackler with a great turn of speed. Rio's also very confident going forward with the ball and became one of the world's most expensive players when he moved from Leeds United to Manchester United for a massive £29.1 million. He made his England debut at the age of 19.

Rio has had his ups and downs with the British press but there's no doubting his heart is in the right place, and he's been a leading figure in anti-bullying campaigns. It's no secret that Rio has his eye on a role in TV when he finally hangs up his boots. Before the last World Cup he hosted 'Rio's World Cup Wind-Ups', which involved playing practical jokes on his famous footballing friends.

Getty Images Sport/Getty Images

Getty Images Sport/Getty Images

Gary Neville

Born: 18.02.75, Bury

Club side: Manchester United FC

Position: Full-back

Debut: v Japan, 03.06.95

Caps: 85

'Gaz' seems to have been around forever! He's now a hugely experienced full-back who gets more reliable with every game he plays. In fact, he's now won more caps than any other England right-back. If England do well by the time the 2008 European Championship draws to a close, there's every chance Gary could have joined an elite band of players with over 100 caps.

He's a player who also loves getting forward and he can whip in a fantastic cross from out wide. Off the pitch, Gary was David Beckham's best man when he married Victoria, while his sister, Tracey, used to play netball for England.

ENGLAND

Getty Images Sport/Getty Images

John Terry

Born: 07.12.80, Barking

Club side: Chelsea FC

Position: Centre-back

Debut: v Serbia & Montenegro, 03.06.03

Caps: 37

John Terry is a natural born leader, the kind of player that everyone wants on their team. He's the solid rock at the heart of the England and Chelsea defence. Fantastic in the air and an aggressive tackler, not many centre-forwards ever get the better of him.

He also scores his fair share of goals and is often seen charging into the box when England have a corner or a free kick in a dangerous position. It comes as a bit of a surprise then, that such a tough footballer is so superstitious! He admits to well over 20 little rituals that are a vital part of his pre-match routine! They involve everything from listening to the same music on the way to the ground, to winding tape round his shin-pads exactly three times.

Jonathan Woodgate

Born: 22.01.80, Middlesbrough

Club side: Real Madrid, Spain

Position: Centre-back

Debut: v Bulgaria, 09.06.99

Caps: 6

OK, let's be honest, Jonathan's time at Real Madrid wasn't the greatest. Not only did he manage to score an own-goal on his debut, but he also got a red card in the same game. "I just can't believe I got sent off," he said at the time. "It's not the best start in the world." Quite, Jonathan, quite!

Now settled back in his home town, Jonathan's playing the best football of his career. He made his name at Leeds United before moving to Newcastle United and then to Spain, although injuries ruined his chances of making it at Real Madrid. A world-class defender who's time may finally have come.

Action Images – Reuters

Player Profiles

Ben Foster

Born: 03.04.83, Leamington Spa

Club side: Manchester United FC

Position: Goalkeeper

Debut: v Spain, 07.02.07

Caps: 1

It's been a mad couple of years for 6ft 2in Ben Foster! He joined Manchester United from Stoke City in July 2005 before he'd even made a first-team appearance at the Britannia Stadium – that's how much he impressed Sir Alex Ferguson, a man who knows a thing or two about football!

Before he'd even had time to say 'hello' to his new teammates, Ben was out on loan at Watford, learning the ropes and helping the Hornets to promotion at the same time!

Ben's an extremely confident keeper and he's already made a name for himself as an excellent shot-stopper.

Getty Images Sport/Getty Images

Paul Robinson

Action Images – Reuters

Born: 15.10.79, Beverley

Club side: Tottenham Hotspur FC

Position: Goalkeeper

Debut: v Australia, 12.02.03

Caps: 34

England has a long tradition of producing great goalkeepers – and Paul Robinson is no exception. He's a huge presence between the posts and is now established as England's Number One. He brilliantly combines great physical strength with bravery and, for such a big fella, impressive agility too.

He recently kept six clean sheets on the trot for England, in the games against Ecuador, Portugal, Greece, Macedonia (twice) and Andorra. Mind you he's had plenty of practice playing in nets. "When I was a kid I used to love playing football; I started playing very young, maybe at six or seven," he says. "I had a go in goal at that sort of age and it was just a case of sticking to what I was good at."

ENGLAND

Skills

From warming up to
free kicks, passing
the ball to the secrets
behind a great tackle,
this section's full of
tips on how to improve
your game.

Warm-Up

Millions of us live it and breathe it. When we're not watching our heroes, we're out there trying to play just like them. Whether it's a real match or a kickabout with some friends, we'd all love to score slick goals like Wayne Rooney, defend as strongly as John Terry or pass like Frank Lampard.

Every player has to start with the basics, and that means practising all the key skills like passing, shooting, defending so you're at the top of your game when it comes to a match.

The Warm-Up

Footballers are an impatient lot. Whether it's just a kickabout in the park or a full-on match, they are always desperate to begin play. But wait. Football is a very active sport and you're less likely to play at your best – and more likely to get injured – if you don't warm up your muscles before play begins.

This is especially important in cold weather, although as young players you aren't quite so vulnerable to muscle strains and injuries. So get into good habits early on and make a thorough warm-up part of your pre-match routine.

The warm-up does two important things. It gets the heart pumping and the blood moving around your body and it prepares the muscles for all that explosive activity on the pitch.

Jog first

A gentle jog is always a good place to start. You can build up the pace slowly, perhaps varying the length of your stride or raising your knees high, skipping or flicking your legs up behind you so that your heels touch your bottom.

Warm-Up

Stretching

Football is a running game. A top player may run up to 12 kilometres in a single match.

So it is important to stretch all your leg muscles before the whistle blows!

Calf

The calf is the muscle at the back of the lower leg.

Stand with one foot in front of the other. Keeping the back leg straight and the body as upright as possible, bend your front leg and move your weight forwards. Hold the position for 20 seconds.

Hamstring

The hamstring is the powerful muscle at the back of the thigh.

Stretch slowly down your body until you feel your hamstring tighten, then hold for 20 seconds.

Quadriceps

The quadriceps is the large muscle at the front of the thigh. Adopting the position shown on the left, hold your ankle and pull it towards your bottom.

Make sure you are well-balanced. If you need more support, you can also use a wall or goalpost to keep you steady.

Hold for 20 seconds and repeat three times with each leg.

Groin

Stand with legs wide apart, feet pointing ahead. Bend forward over one leg then the other, keeping them both straight.

Warm Down

After a game or training session, it is also important to 'warm down'. Stretching all your muscle groups helps prevent them from stiffening up.

Striking the Ball

The ball can be struck with the inside or outside of the foot, the instep, the heel and even the toe occasionally.

Every situation is different.

The push pass

The ball is simply stroked along the ground using the inside of the foot, known as the push pass. The large surface area of the boot that touches the ball makes it very accurate and reliable over short distances.

- The inside of the foot strikes the ball so that it is at right angles to the intended direction of the pass.

- The non-striking foot should be level with the ball.

- Weight should be over the ball on point of impact.

- The head should be steady, with eyes on the ball.

- The ball should be struck through its horizontal midline.

- The foot follows through in the direction of the pass.

Swerving the ball

Striking the ball off-centre will give it sidespin and make it travel in an arc rather than in a straight line.

Using the inside of the foot

Practise bending the ball with the inside of the foot first, as it is easier to control.

Strike across the right-hand side of the ball about halfway up (the left side if you are left-footed). As your foot makes contact it should rotate slightly, wrapping around the ball.

Using the outside of the foot

Striking the left-hand side of the ball with the outside of the boot will bend it from left to right. Toes should be pointing down at point of contact. A long follow-through is very important.

ENGLAND

The drive

When driving the ball, timing is much more important than brute force.

The lofted (upward) drive – great for long passing

- Your standing leg should be slightly behind the ball.

- The toes should be pointing down on contact with the ball.

- Hit through the centre of the ball, but this time below the midpoint. Follow through.

The low drive – ideal when shooting

- Place your standing leg alongside the ball.

- Strike the ball with the toes pointing down.

- Hit through the centre of the ball, and follow through.

- Your body weight should be over the ball.

- Timing is more important than force and will help to keep the ball down.

When power and distance are called for, the ball should be driven with the instep.

Striking the Ball

The volley

If the ball comes to you in the air, you can either control it or strike (volley) it first time.

The power volley

Volleys can be hit hard to generate a lot of power and speed. For a front-on power volley, take your leg back, lift your knee and stretch your ankle with toes pointing down as the ball arrives. Keep your head forward and your body over the ball so it stays low. Leaning back a little will send the ball up higher, which can be of use when defending and clearing the ball from your penalty area.

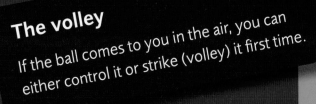

The side volley

Make sure you are well-balanced on your standing leg. This is particularly important for a waist-high volley, when it is easy to fall away as you strike the ball. The body rotates around the standing leg as you make contact with the ball.

The controlled volley

This sees the ball hit relatively gently with either the sidefoot or instep and used for a close shot or short pass to a teammate.

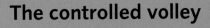

Strike the centre of the ball with the instep. Aim to make contact too high rather than too low, especially when shooting. If you get underneath the ball, it will balloon up in the air and over the bar. On the other hand, if you get over the ball, it will lose some of its pace but it still might be enough to beat the keeper.

The chip

Players often find themselves needing to get the ball up and over an opponent but down quickly behind them. The chip shot sees the ball rise steeply but dip down sharply as it falls. On landing, the backspin on the ball stops it from racing away. The chip is useful for getting the ball over a keeper who is off his line, but down in time to enter the goal.

The non-kicking foot should be close to the ball, the knees slightly bent. The instep of the striking foot stabs down under the ball, and should make contact with the ball and the ground at the same time. There should be minimal follow-through. The chip is much easier with a stationary ball or one rolling towards you. It is more difficult if the ball is moving away from you.

Passing

Passing links the players in a team and can turn defence into attack. When passing to a teammate, the sidefoot pass is the most accurate pass, and good over short to medium distances.

When you have the ball, you should have a choice of players to pass to. You must decide which is the right option. Forward passes are essential to build an attack, but a sideways or backwards pass can be good if it keeps possession and changes the point of the attack.

Passes on the ground can often be delivered more accurately than passes in the air and are easier for the receiver to control. Passes in the air can give defenders more time to intercept but they can also help to launch a quick attack.

The weight of a pass is the amount of force with which it is hit and the speed with which it travels away. And only practice makes perfect!

Many passes are aimed straight at the teammate, but sometimes a pass needs to be made to one side so that the receiver of the pass can cut away from their opponent to collect the ball. Other passes are aimed into space ahead of a speedy attacker.

Receiving the Ball

A good pass puts the ball within easy reach of the receiver. But poor passes have to be received, too, so players need lots of practice in receiving balls that are spinning, bouncing awkwardly, travelling at great pace or coming at a difficult height.

Before the ball arrives, you should already have decided whether you are going to strike it first time or bring it under control. The less time you spend controlling the ball, the more you have to line up an accurate pass, shot or run forward. A player's first touch of the ball, whether it is with the thigh, foot or chest, is often crucial.

Cushion control

The object with cushion control is to kill the ball's speed and keep it within your own playing distance. If you allow the ball to cannon off you and rebound a couple of metres away, then the ball is loose and could be pounced on by the opposition. The part of your body making contact with the ball must be relaxed and must be moved away from the ball as it arrives to deaden its impact and leave it, usually, at your feet. Care should be taken to avoid contact with the arms.

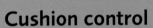

Firm control

Sometimes, players choose to keep some of the pace on the ball but change its direction.

Firm control can allow you to make an instant short pass to a teammate or propel the ball ahead of you to run on to. The surface touching the ball should be held relatively firm and thrust forward on impact, for example, when you want to keep the ball moving ahead of you.

Often a player will want to take a high ball on the chest and push it into the space in front of him to run on to. Here, the chest is pushed out at the point of impact.

Keep the chest firm to steer the ball into space or pass to a teammate. Keep your arms and hands well away from the ball.

ENGLAND

Controlling the ball

Getting in line

Whether you choose cushion or firm control, the same rules apply. Decide which part of the body you're going to use to receive the ball as early as possible. Get your body in line with the ball. Go and meet the ball, don't wait for it to arrive. Use your body to shield the ball from your marker. Keep your eyes on the ball, but try to be aware of what is going on around you before the ball arrives. This is hard and only comes with experience and lots of practice.

Side of the foot

This is the most popular and effective way to control the ball. The broadest area of the foot meets the middle of the ball, bringing it to rest just in front of the player. The leg is moved back along the line of the ball's flight to take the pace off the ball and bring it to rest.

Receiving the Ball

Sole of the foot

Trapping the ball this way will bring it to a standstill. It requires perfect timing to ensure the ball doesn't bounce off the foot or slide underneath it.

Don't stamp down on the ball hard or it may squirt out from under your foot. The position of the foot is the same as for a sidefoot pass.

Instep

Only use this when it is impossible to get into the correct position with the side of the foot. With less surface area in contact with the ball, there is more chance of the ball bouncing too far away or going off at an angle.

Top of the foot

This is only used when a ball is dropping from a height. The ball should be cushioned as the foot drops to the floor with the ball.

Thigh control

Lower the leg to cushion the ball as it makes contact. This will bring the ball to rest at your feet instead of bouncing out of control.

Shielding the ball

Sometimes you will have the luxury of being able to receive the ball or play it while in plenty of space. More often you will have an opponent closing you down and looking for an opportunity to challenge. This is when screening or shielding the ball comes into its own. Quite simply, the golden rule is to keep your body between your opponent and the ball, thereby making it much more difficult for him or her to make a tackle without committing a foul.

To shield the ball, position your body between the ball and your opponent. Keep the ball under close control.

Be aware of where your opponent is and keep moving to ensure that your body stays between them and the ball.

You must not back into or push your opponent, but you can keep your arms out for balance. Look for your next move, whether it is a turn and sprint with the ball or a pass sideways or backwards.

Shooting

Football is all about scoring goals. Teams that don't make many attempts on goal are far more likely to struggle.

It is important to be aware of teammates in better positions than you, but don't pass on the ball and the responsibility when you get a good goal-scoring chance. If an opportunity to shoot arises, and it is within your range, then go for it.

Shooting checklist

Be aware

Keep your head up and your mind on the game. This will help you spot and react well to shooting chances.

Be confident

Don't be afraid of failure. If you do miss, put it straight out of your mind and be just as confident the next time.

Be quick

Chances come and go in an instant. Don't hesitate or take one touch too many; this can result in a good chance being lost.

Go low

Aiming high for a thundering shot towards the top corner of the goal may look spectacular, but such a shot is often saved as it arrives at a good height for a goalkeeper – or it may miss altogether. A low shot into the corner or into an empty part of the goal is often more effective, and may also lead to a deflection.

Placement versus power

For close-range shooting, accuracy comes first, power second. Shots hit from further out need more power, but even here, you should concentrate on a smooth swing of your foot rather than trying to smash the ball.

ENGLAND

Use both feet

If defenders know you will only go for goal with your stronger foot, they will cover that side and make shooting difficult. Work hard on shooting well with both feet so that you offer double the threat and can shoot from both sides.

Anticipate

Good strikers seem to know instinctively where the ball will fall, and position themselves accordingly. Even if you haven't reached that level yet, try to guess the outcome: will a teammate win a header or will the ball bounce off the goalposts or the goalkeeper and reach you?

Set pieces

Throw-ins, corners, free kicks and penalties have two major advantages. First, the player taking the kick or throw is dealing with a ball that's not moving! Second, set pieces can be practised at training and your teammates should know exactly what is going to happen.

And be alert – a quick set piece can catch defenders off guard.

Defending set pieces

Players take their instructions from their goalkeeper. The penalty area can get crowded, and defenders need to stay fully focused and ready to react to a quick move by the player they are marking.

At set pieces defenders should try to position themselves so that they can see both the player they are marking and the ball.

Corners

Corners can be taken short or long, and can be delivered to the far post, near post or middle of the goal. They can be bent inwards (inswing) or hit so that they bend outwards (outswing). Much depends on the corner taker to deliver an accurate ball at the right height and into the right area for his team. His teammates then have to time their runs and jumps and get free of their marker to make contact with the ball.

Free kicks

When it comes to deciding whether to shoot (assuming that it's a direct free kick), the distance from goal and the angle will be the deciding factors. If the kick is too wide or too far out, then you should aim to get the ball into the danger area. Generally, that means playing the ball behind the last defender. Defenders like to play the ball in front of them; they hate turning and having to defend while facing their own goal, particularly if under pressure.

66

Choosing to shoot

For more central free kicks that are within striking range, the defending side have even more to worry about. They will usually put up a wall to give the goalkeeper extra protection.

Penalties

A penalty is an excellent chance of scoring; although the penalty taker has a better chance of scoring than the keeper has of saving, there is still work to be done.

A penalty taker has a number of choices to make about where to hit the ball. Some players prefer power, and choose to blast the ball with an instep drive aimed at the middle of the goal. Others prefer to place the ball using a controlled instep drive or firm sidefoot shot low into the corners of the net.

Throw-ins

Bend your knees and arch your back while keeping good balance.

Take the ball right back over your head.

Release the ball as it passes in front of your head.

Spread your hands around the back and sides of the ball so that your thumbs almost touch. This gives you good grip of the football.

Remember you must keep both feet on the ground, otherwise it's a foul throw.

As soon as you have taken a throw-in, step back onto the pitch and be alert. Sometimes, the person who receives the throw may look to pass the ball straight back to you.

Make life as easy as possible for the receiver. Your teammate won't appreciate a ball bouncing awkwardly, or delivered where their marker can easily challenge.

Dribbling

Dribbling is all about using close control skills with the ball to take on and beat one or more opponents. But it's better to dribble past one player and then release a good pass than to beat three players only to lose the ball to the fourth.

It can be a risky business, so best to save your dribbling for the attacking third of the pitch.

Turning

Being able to turn quickly with the ball under control can help a player beat an opponent or get an attacker to face goal ready to shoot. You can change your direction by running around the ball or standing on one foot and pivoting around with the other – but don't forget the ball!

Successful dribbling

Most players have a stronger leg, but if you always use that one to play the ball, the defender will know what to expect from you. Don't try to beat a defender on the same side every time either. The more you can keep your opponent guessing, the better your chances will be of getting past him or her.

Keep the ball under close control

Kicking the ball too far ahead makes the defender's job easy.

Keep your head up

This means you can keep an eye on the whereabouts of your teammates and opponents.

Attack with pace

An opponent running at pace with the ball under control is a defender's nightmare. If you're not very fast, try to vary your pace to keep the defender guessing.

Change direction

Twist and turn to keep a defender on their toes. The more often they have to change their stride, the more chance you have of putting them off balance.

Shield the ball

Whenever possible, keep your body between the defender and the ball. This will make it harder for them to take the ball without committing a foul.

Feinting

Feinting involves fooling your opponent into thinking you are going to go one way, then moving off in a completely different direction. You can do this in a lot of ways, but the common element in all cases is the use of exaggerated body movements. Defenders are supposed to concentrate on the ball, not on the movement of the body, but even the best defenders will react to body movements. Trying to fool a defender in this way is also known as 'selling a dummy'.

Dropping the shoulder

1. As you approach the defender, throw your body weight to the left to make it look as if you are going to move in that direction.

2. An exaggerated drop of your left shoulder fools the defender into thinking you plan to go that way.

3. As the defender reacts, swerve in the opposite direction and accelerate past him on the right.

Heading

Football purists often say that the game is supposed to be played on the ground, not up in the air. They don't like to see a lot of aerial 'ping-pong'. But sometimes a high ball is exactly the right option to choose.

Once the ball is in the air, both teams will want to challenge for it. If you wait for the ball to drop, you run the risk of losing possession, or maybe even allowing the other team to score a goal. No matter what the purists say, heading is a skill that can win and lose games.

Heading a ball doesn't come naturally to some young players, but can be learned and practised. You don't have to be tall to be good in the air; timing, technique and having good 'spring' are the most important factors.

Use your forehead

By making contact with the ball above the eyes you will be able to watch the ball right up to the moment of impact. It will make controlling the direction of the header easier and, done well, won't hurt.

Keep your eyes open

Photographs show that even professionals close their eyes at the precise moment of contact between head and ball. This is normal, but you should try to keep your eyes on the ball for as long as possible.

Arch your back, nod your head

In many cases, you will be trying to get maximum power into your header. By arching your back and snapping forward at the point of contact, you will give your head forward momentum when it meets the ball. Even more power is generated if you also use your neck muscles to punch through the ball at the same time.

Attack the ball

Be positive, be first to the ball. Meet the ball and don't let it hit you. If you wait, the chance of an opponent getting to it first increases.

ENGLAND

Different types of header

1. Defensive header

This header is used for clearing the ball away from your goal and out of danger. You are aiming for maximum power to head the ball up but mainly forwards to get it as far away as possible. Try to make contact just below the middle of the ball.

2. Heading for goal

Accuracy is vital with an attacking header. Getting above the ball to head it down is crucial. Not only does that help prevent the ball from sailing over the crossbar, it can also be harder for a keeper to save. Aim to connect just above the middle of the ball.

Diving headers can be very effective as well as spectacular. If you launch yourself at the ball, a header can be as powerful as a kick.

3. Cushioned header

This is used when passing back to your goalkeeper or when you want to set up a teammate nearby. The key thing is to relax your neck and shoulder muscles and to bring your head back as you connect with the ball. Your aim should be to remove most of the ball's speed as it travels gently to your teammate.

Defending

Defending involves decision-making and taking up positions that will help your team win the ball or prevent your opponents from using it to their advantage.

And it's not just for defenders! When the opposition are in possession, good teams defend from the front. This means that strikers should be the first players to pressure their opponents with the ball.

Defenders often mark an opponent closely to deny him or her the space to receive the pass. As a defender you must try and stay between the opponent and your own goal to make it harder for the opponent to shoot.

Prevent your opponent from turning

A player receiving the ball will be a greater attacking threat if allowed to turn. As a defender, you should react quickly and aim to get within one metre of your opponent by the time the ball arrives. If you hang back any further, the attacker will have room to manoeuvre into a good position to pass, dribble or shoot. If you get too close, it will be difficult to keep the ball in view, and a quick move from the attacker could take him or her out of range before you have time to react.

Jockeying

Even if the attacker has been able to turn, it is still up to them to do something with the ball. Don't dive in unnecessarily and solve the problem for them. Be patient and wait for a momentary loss of control, when the odds will be stacked in your favour to win the ball.

Standing on the balls of his feet, the defender jockeys his opponent. His body weight is over his knees, which are flexed. He is ready to move in any direction and keeps a distance between himself and his opponent. He watches the ball closely.

A defender may also try to jockey their opponent across field or to the sidelines and away from good attacking positions. In doing so, the defender may also buy their teammates extra time to get back into good defensive positions.

ENGLAND

Tackling

Tackling is all about winning the ball cleanly from an opponent.

Watch the ball, not the player.

Keep moving yourself into the best position while you are waiting for the right moment to strike. This includes using your body position to manoeuvre your opponents into less dangerous areas.

When you decide to make a tackle, the important factors are speed, determination, accuracy and timing. If your tackle is clumsy you risk fouling your opponent and giving away a free kick or penalty.

Interceptions

Be alert for an under-hit or misdirected pass. If you can steal the ball before it reaches the intended receiver, you won't need to tackle him.

The block tackle

The block tackle is the most common challenge in football.

When you arrive at the ball at the same time as your opponent, first ensure a good body position with your weight over the ball.

1. To win the ball, you must get as much of your foot in contact with it as possible. Your full body weight should drive through the tackling leg.

2. If the ball gets stuck, push the ball and roll it up and over the top of your opponent's foot.

The slide tackle

When tackling, try to stay on your feet. Once you go to ground, you are out of the game. Only commit to a slide tackle if you are certain of winning the challenge. The reason for this is that most slide tackles are made from behind and are risky.

You must make sure that you do not hit the attacker's leg before connecting with the ball, or the referee may give a free kick or penalty. Most players try to use the leg furthest away from the attacker to make the tackle as this gives you more balance and a stronger tackling position. If the timing is perfect, you can hook your foot around the ball and cradle it there throughout the tackle to keep possession. The aim with many slide tackles, though, is to remove the ball from the opponent's control and out of play.

Goalkeeping

As the last line of defence, goalkeepers can grab the glory, but are also under a lot of pressure. Brilliant saves can win games, but mistakes are often punished and can lose games as well.

Agility to make dives and leaps, fast reactions and excellent handling skills are all things a good goalkeeper needs. Goalkeepers must also be brave and need strong powers of concentration. They may be asked to do nothing for a long period then suddenly pull off a spectacular save or face a high-pressure one-on-one situation.

Goalkeepers can often help protect their goal without making a save. They do this through communicating with their defenders and directing them clearly. Staying alert and aware, the keeper often has the best view of an opposition attack.

A keeper who makes quick, clear decisions and communicates orders well to his defenders is said to be in command of his penalty area.

Shot stopping

As a goalkeeper, you should get as much of your body as possible behind the ball. Two hands are therefore better than one, and if the body is behind the hands to provide a second barrier, all the better. Of course, this isn't always possible and getting anything behind the ball is important. This might be a hand, the fingertips, or even an outstretched leg.

Ready position

A goalkeeper's ready position sees you well-balanced on the balls of your feet and ready to move quickly in any direction. Hands should be held out at about waist height and eyes should be on the game ahead.

Shots along the ground

For shots along the ground most keepers tend to drop one knee and scoop up the ball with both hands. Others bend their back and stoop to take the ball.

Low shots

For shots between knee and waist height, get the body behind the ball and use the scooping technique to bring it into the chest. If the shot is low, the body will naturally topple forward, but the ball will be safely cupped to the chest before you hit the ground.

Shots at chest height

There are two techniques. The first is to cup your hands underneath the ball and bend your body to clutch the ball into your chest.

For the second method, catch the ball with your fingers spread out and away from your body. In both cases, keep your hands and fingers flexible so that they cushion the impact of the ball.

Taking high balls

Catch the ball at the highest possible point. The lower it drops, the more vulnerable you will be to a challenge. Maximum height will be gained with a one-footed take-off. The fingers should be spread wide and not too tense. Once the ball is in your hands, bring it down and into the chest as soon as possible.

Goalkeeping

Diving

For shots wide of the keeper, where you are unable to get your body behind the ball, you may have to launch yourself to make a save. Push off with the leg nearest the ball and aim to get both hands on it if possible.

Catch, punch or deflect?

Catching the ball is best, but sometimes it may not be possible. If you are under pressure, a very firm punch, one- or two-handed, and through the middle of the ball, can send it out of danger.

Be careful, though, of simply punching it back to the opposition. A deflection can stop a goal by guiding the ball round the post or over the bar. To deflect the ball, make contact with the open palm and outstretched fingers. Guide the ball over the bar or round the post. Take care not to get too full and firm a contact, as the ball might rebound back into danger.

ENGLAND

Positional play

Goalkeepers should be constantly changing their position depending on where the ball is. When possible, the keeper should place him- or herself in a direct line between the ball and the centre of the goal.

As well as moving to the left or right, the goalkeeper also has to be ready to go forwards. If an attacker is 'through on goal', as keeper you must aim to make yourself as big an obstacle as possible. At the same time, you will be limiting the attacker's view of the goal.

Narrowing the angle is one of a keeper's range of vital weapons, but it isn't risk-free. If you advance too far or not far enough, too soon or too late, you will give the advantage to the attacker. The attacker might then pass, dribble past or go for a chip.

Always make sure you have a good view of the ball. From free kicks it is often best to get a good view of your opponent kicking the ball rather than have your vision completely hidden by the defending wall.

Good positioning can make difficult saves look quite easy. Being in the right place at the right time is perhaps the goalkeeper's most important skill, and probably the most difficult to learn. Good judgement only comes with experience and lots of work in training.

Distribution

The decision-making doesn't stop once a keeper has possession of the ball. He or she has to choose how to release the ball and distribute it to their team. Good decision-making and fast, accurate distribution can turn defence into attack.

Keepers have a choice of short underarm throws or more powerful overarm and 'javelin' throws. They can also kick the ball from their hand to gain maximum distance.

Keepers also have to be good at kicking a rolling ball because of the backpass rule, which stops them from picking up a ball deliberately passed back to them.

Frank Lampard playing for England against Spain in February 2007

We kick off this section with a look back at the highs and the lows of nearly 80 years of international football at Wembley. Then it's a close-up look at six of the most thrilling England games of all time. Is your favourite among them?

Wembley is the home of English football. It staged its first international match in April 1924, fittingly against Scotland, and its last in 2000 against Germany. It was demolished three years later, and now a new Wembley has been built, a stadium which is among the best in the world.

Wembley

Open the gates!

Wembley was first opened in 1923 and known as the Empire Stadium. The first football match there was the 1923 FA Cup Final between West Ham United and Bolton, and it became known as the White Horse Final. So many people flocked into the ground that mounted police had to clear the pitch. And one of those horses was a white one called Billy!

The first ten England internationals at Wembley were all against Scotland! Teams didn't travel abroad as much in those days. So little surprise then that it was Scotland who were the first team to beat England at Wembley. In 1928 a Scotland team who became known as the Wembley Wizards won 5-1.

England have twice scored nine goals at Wembley. In 1961 they thrashed Scotland 9-3, with Jimmy Greaves (pictured below) scoring a hat-trick. And then in 1982 they beat Luxembourg 9-0, with Luther Blissett England's three-goal hero this time around.

Hulton Archive/Getty Images

Hungary have a feast!

In 1953, Hungary became the first team from continental Europe to win at Wembley. This fantastic team – nicknamed the Magical Magyars – beat England 6-3. The picture shows the two teams being led out. The England skipper (in white) is Billy Wright; the Hungarian captain is a famous player called Ferenc Puskas.

Hulton Archive/Getty Images

Number one Fan!

A great colour snap from the 1966 World Cup Final, with one of Wembley's famous towers in the background. The man in the picture is England's 'no.1 supporter' Ken Bailey, who hardly ever missed an England game. He became a bit of an official mascot, and would even walk out with the team sometimes!

World Cup Winners

England parade the World Cup around Wembley after their win 4-2 against West Germany in 1966.

This is a famous selection of pictures showing Geoff Hurst celebrating the winning goal against Argentina in the World Cup quarter-final in 1966.

Wembley

Stuart Pearce looks relieved after scoring his penalty in the shoot-out against Spain at Euro 96.

Record attendances

On no fewer than 13 occasions, 100,000 people have crammed into Wembley to watch England play. It was only after more seats were added that the ground's capacity dropped – and so did the size of the crowds.

England v Austria - Nov 28 1951

England v Hungary - Nov 25 1953

England v West Germany - Dec 1 1954

England v USSR - Oct 22 1958

England v Portugal - Oct 25 1961

England v Rest of the World - Oct 23 1963

England v Spain - Apr 3 1968

England v Portugal - Dec 10 1969

England v Northern Ireland - Apr 21 1970

England v West Germany - Apr 29 1972

England v Poland - Oct 17 1973

England v West Germany - Mar 12 1975

England v Scotland - May 26 1979

During the 1970s England and Scotland had many great games. Here England's Dave Watson uses Scotland's Kenny Dalglish to get a bit of extra lift. Scotland went on to win this one 2-1.

Hulton Archive/Getty Images

Getty Images Sport/Getty Images

This is how Wembley looked from the air just before an England v Scotland game at Euro 96. And most of the 77,000 crowd went home happy, as England won 2-0.

England fans

Getty Images Sport/Getty Images

The roar of England fans at Wembley has often helped lift the team on the pitch. And many players have talked about the tingling feeling they get as they walked out of the tunnel behind the goal for the first time. Let's hope the new Wembley has the same effect!

End of the road

Getty Images Sport/Getty Images

England fans make their way to the famous old ground for the last time before a World Cup qualifier against Germany in 2000.

Here are ten weird and wonderful facts about Wembley

21. If you placed all 90,000 seats at the new Wembley end to end, they'd stretch 54km.

12. Need the loo? No worries, Wembley now has precisely 2,618 toilets – which, it's claimed, is more than any other building in the world.

13. Each of the two giant screens in the new stadium is the size of 600 standard tellies like the one in your front room.

14. You could fit the London Eye in between the top of the new arch and the pitch.

15. If you ran all around the outside of Wembley you'd have completed 1km.

16. Right, are you paying attention! The new Wembley encloses 4,000,000 m3 (cubic metres) inside its walls and under its roof. If that doesn't mean much to you, then try this. That's enough space to fit 25,000 double decker buses, or 7 billion pints of milk!

17. The old Wembley cost £750,000 to build. The new one is slightly more expensive at an estimated £750 million!

18. Wembley became England's permanent home in January 1966.

19. Wembley was also used for many other football events, such as The FA Cup Final, while just after the war it also hosted the 1948 Olympics. And in 1985 the Live Aid concert was staged there.

10. In 1999, Paul Scholes was the first player to be sent off while playing for England at home. He got his marching orders against Sweden.

Who's playing?

England v West Germany.

What's so special?

It's the one and only time that England have won the World Cup.

What was the score?

England won 4-2 after extra time.

Geoff Hurst shoots towards the German goal. But did it go in?

Job done! Bobby Moore kisses the famous gold trophy.

Hulton Archive/Getty Images

When it came to extra time it all got very controversial! A shot by Hurst hit the underside of the bar and bounced down. But did it cross the goal line? The ref asked the linesman. They had a brief chat and then the ref pointed towards the centre circle. Goal! England were 3-2 up!

This time, the Germans failed to come. Hurst became the first player to score a hat-trick (three goals) in a World Cup Final with the last kick of the match. England were World Champions.

It was a right ding-dong game. Germany started off as slight favourites, so it was no surprise when they took the lead after just 12 minutes. But England were soon back in it, Geoff Hurst heading home a free kick from the England skipper Bobby Moore. And it stayed at 1-1 until 12 minutes from the end.

Martin Peters then put England back into the lead, tapping home from close range. The Wembley crowd went mad. But then disaster struck. Germany won a free kick, the ball cannoned off the wall and fell kindly to the German Wolfgang Weber who slotted it past the England keeper Gordon Banks.

World Champions! England's triumphant cup-winning team. With the Jules Rimet Trophy are (back row, left to right) Harold Shepherdson (trainer) Nobby Stiles, Roger Hunt, Gordon Banks, Jackie Charlton, George Cohen Ray Wilson and manager Alf Ramsey; (front row) Martin Peters, Geoff Hurst

ENGLAND

The occasion:

World Cup quarter-final, July 1, 1990.

Who's playing?

England against Cameroon, the surprise package of Italia 90.

Gary Lineker is sent crashing for the first penalty.

Gary Lineker is tripped by Cameroon's goalkeeper Thomas Nkono.

David Platt scored the only goal of the first half, heading home a Stuart Pearce cross. But although Cameroon had plenty of chances to draw level, Peter Shilton and the rest of the England defence just about stood firm.

When it came to penalties, England were under siege at the start of the second half and finally cracked, Paul Gascoigne fouling Roger Milla in the box. The penalty was scored for 1-1. England began to look a bit creaky and within five minutes the Africans were ahead 2-1.

Things were not going to plan at all. England were being over-run in midfield and half the defence was limping. Time was ticking away.

So what did we do? Looked to Gary Lineker, who else! With seven minutes left he surged into the box but was sent flying. Penalty! Up stepped Lineker and bang! it was 2-2 and extra time.

It ended with a fantastic finish. Gazza splits the defence with a perfect pass, Lineker runs into the box and BANG, the Cameroon keeper runs out to meet him! Penalty number 3. Once again the team's hopes rested with Lineker. Will he blast it or place? Go right or left? Well, he went for straight down the middle... but the keeper went to his right! 3-2 to England.

Well done Gary – England draw level at 2-2.

Great games - Germany 1996

The occasion:

European Championship semi-final, Wembley, June 26, 1996.

Who's playing?

England and Germany of course!

What's so special?

England are on the verge of their first Final for thirty years.

Alan Shearer opens the scoring for England.

Paul Gascoigne launches another England attack.

At the start, England got off to an absolute flyer when Alan Shearer headed home a near-post corner after just two minutes!

It looked like it was going downhill after that... Germany equalised just over ten minutes later. It was a right ding-dong battle after that but there were no more goals and the game went to extra time and Golden Goals, with the next team to score the winners!

First Darren Anderton was inches away with a shot that flew across the face of the goal. Then moments later Stefan Kuntz scored for Germany at the other end! The 76,000 people who had crammed into Wembley looked at the ref; the ref looked at his linesman; the linesman looked back at him. "No goal," said the man in black. The game was still on!

Suddenly Alan Shearer found himself out on the right wing. Come on, come on...he crossed the ball. Paul Gascoigne slid in...but missed the ball. The ref blew up and it was penalties. This was not good!

Incredibly, England scored the first five but unfortunately so did Germany. So up stepped Gareth Southgate. He ran forward and...hit it straight at the keeper. Cue Andy Möller, who stroked the ball past David Seaman and put Germany into the Final.

More shoot-out frustration for England.

ENGLAND

The occasion:

A group match at the European Championship played at Wembley on June 18, 1996.

Why all the excitement?

It wasn't so much that England won the game, it's they way they played, against one of the tournament favourites, that stood out.

It started as Alan Shearer blasted England ahead from the penalty spot after Paul Ince had been tripped. But it wasn't until the second half that England upped the tempo and began purring like a finely tuned engine...

Alan Shearer puts England ahead from the spot.

But seriously, England were beginning to play some great football. Teddy Sheringham headed in the second goal from a Paul Gascoigne corner but the best was yet to come.

It was that good. Steve McManaman passed to Gascoigne who skipped past a defender before pulling the ball to Sheringham. Everyone thought he was going to shoot but instead he slid the ball across the box to Shearer who smashed home his second. The Brazilians couldn't have done it better!

The Dutch had no answer to Gazza's magic.

Anderton's long shot was saved by the Dutch keeper Edwin Van Der Sar but it squirmed free and Sheringham tucked home the rebound.

So Holland did get one back. And that was enough to see them qualify for the next stage, knocking out Scotland in the process! And that certainly made some England fans even happier.

There's no stopping Alan Shearer.

The occasion:

World Cup qualifier in Munich,
September 1, 2001.

Who's playing?

Germany and England.

Germany have a six-point lead at the
top of the qualifying group for the 2002
World Cup. And only one team are
certain to go through.

That'll be 3-1 then Michael!

England celebrate after Steven Gerrard puts England 2-1 up.

So, six minutes gone and Carsten Jancker gives
Germany the lead.

But then England go on an incredible – and I
mean incredible – scoring spree. First Owen
smashes home a tremendous half volley, and
then Steven Gerrard goes one better, with an
absolute screamer from 30 yards. The England
fans at the ground go barmy!

We were winning at half-time and it wasn't long
before it was 3-1 as the German defence melted
away and Owen bagged his second, after a
knock down from strike partner Emile Heskey.

To good to be true? Well pinch yourself, it gets
even better because Owen completes his hat-
trick. His electric pace leaves the German s
reeling and he skips into the box to make it 4-1!

It was unbelievable! Emile Heskey couldn't
believe it when he made it 5-1. It was
Germany's worst defeat since they lost 6-0 to
Austria in 1930.

Not something you see every day!

ENGLAND

The occasion:

European Championship quarter-final, Lisbon, June 24, 2004.

Who's playing?

England against host nation Portugal.

What's so special?

This is an absolute belter of a game, with more twists and turns than Joe Cole dribbling.

It started unbelievably well for England! David James launched a huge goal kick, Michael Owen controlled the ball brilliantly and then superbly flicked it over the keeper into the back of the net. England were one up with just three minutes gone.

Michael Owen gives England an early lead.

Frank Lampard takes a tumble.

Portugal didn't equalise straight away. England weren't playing that well but they held on until seven minutes from the end. But then Portuguese substitute Helder Postiga sneaked past the England defence to head the ball home.

This meant extra time, but only after Sol Campbell had what every England fan thought was a perfectly good goal ruled out right on the final whistle. Instead it was Portugal that went ahead, this time through a fantastic strike by Rui Costa after 110 minutes.

But it wasn't over yet! Back came England again, with Frank Lampard stabbing the ball home from close range to send the match into penalties.

It did get ugly. David Beckham slipped as he ran up to take the first kick, and sent it over the bar. At 5-5, Ricardo saved well from Darius Vassell and then really rubbed England's noses in it by stepping up to slot home the winner.

The England wall does its job.

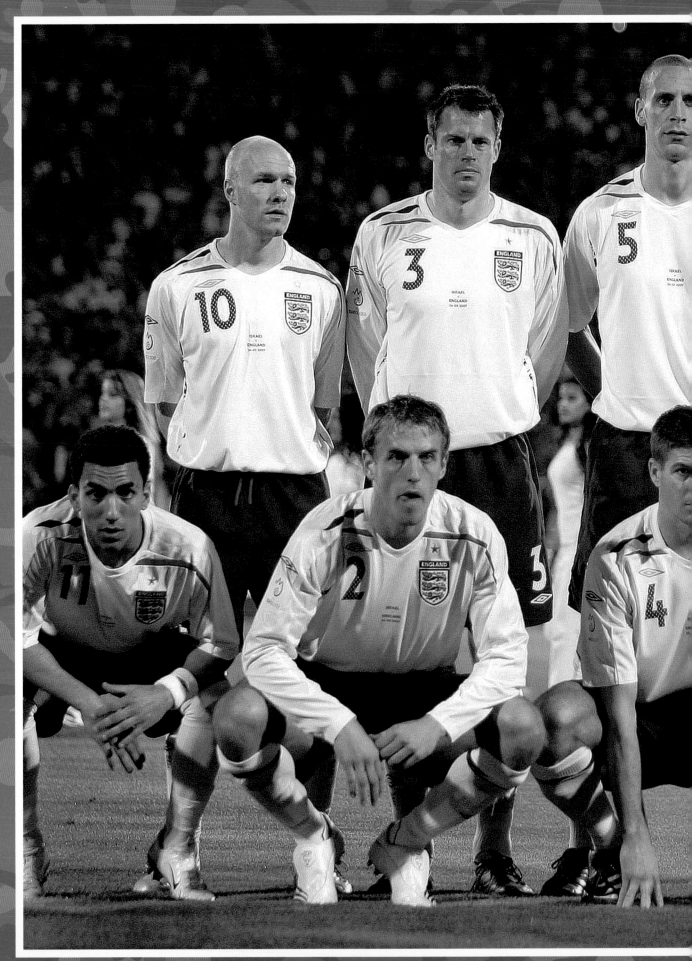

Group line-up Israel v England UEFA Euro 2008 Qualifying Group E, 24 March 2007